Marjorie Bilbow is a well-known film critic and broadcaster.

Published by G. Whizzard Publications Ltd.,
in association with André Deutsch Ltd., 1978
105 Great Russell Street, London W.C.1.

Fact Books © G. Whizzard Publications Ltd., 1978

Text © Marjorie Bilbow 1978

ISBN 0 233 96772 9

Printed by Tien Wah Press (Pte.) Ltd., Singapore

The Facts about a Feature Film
Featuring Hammer Films
Introduction by Christopher Lee

By Marjorie Bilbow
Photographed by John Claridge

Series consultant editor: Alan Road

Introduction

During thirty years as an actor in the film world, I have read many books about the cinema, published in many languages in many countries.

Some of these have been technical, some biographical, some even financial. But this is the first time that I have read any book about the making of a film which so clearly and thoroughly explains what motion pictures really mean, from the point of view of everybody involved, on both sides of the camera.

I congratulate Marjorie Bilbow on the precise and simple way in which she has set out, from beginning to end, what it really feels like to be a part of the whole production. Nobody is ignored or undervalued.

Her book, written with great clarity and indeed affection, sets out to show the general public that the production of a film is not merely a matter of the Package, the Deal, or the Sale; but, more important, the combined efforts of groups of people totally dedicated to their work. And work it is: harder than most professions and frequently underestimated and unrewarded.

Marjorie has always been devoted to the cinema and has, always, been fair in her appraisal and judgments.

I whole-heartedly recommend the reading of this book, which is a 'must' for all in the industry – and a fascinating revelation for the public to enjoy.

Christopher Lee

Foreword

On sale and in libraries there are many books which detail and analyse the work of famous producers, directors, lighting cameramen, art directors, editors, special effects men, etc. And there are numerous textbooks which explain all the technicalities of sound, camera work, dubbing, film processing and so on.

This book does not attempt to include every detail of every facet of film making. Its purpose is to explain how films are made by a team of people all pulling together.

All films are made in much the same way, but no two films are made identically.

If films were made by robots programmed to make films according to set rules, the process would never change and a factual description of it would not be scattered with 'ifs' and 'buts' and 'maybes'. Every film would be of equal standard, never disappointing but never excitingly different.

It is the sudden flash of inspiration, the extra effort needed to overcome an unexpected problem, the different personalities all giving something of themselves, that give films their individuality.

This is why one particular film has been used to illustrate how the basic principles of film making were applied by the team of people brought together to make it.

To the Devil . . . A Daughter was chosen as an example of a medium budget production made for the entertainment of cinemagoers all over the world that also made special demands on the cast, director and crew to create an atmosphere of mixed realism and fantasy.

The problems that had to be solved were particular to the film, yet typical of the sort of problems that crop up every time a group of people get together to perform the miracle of bringing words on paper to the screen as an experience to be shared by millions.

Marjorie Bilbow

Action!

Screenplay

'In the beginning was the Word.' That quotation from the Bible is the motto of The Writer's Guild of Great Britain, and a very appropriate choice it is. Or should be. All too often the writer of a screenplay will see his work totally changed when the film reaches the screen. Sometimes this is necessary, sometimes not, because personal opinions are involved and opinions can be wrong. The name or names that appear in the credit titles are not always to be relied on. Other writers may have been called in to make changes; directors often re-write, and stars may insist on altering their own lines.

There is no one way for a film to get a script, or for a script to end up as a film. A producer may think of an idea and raise money on the strength of it and the star names he has (or pretends he has!) lined up. Having raised the money, he will then employ a writer to produce a screenplay. If the result isn't what he had in mind, he may get another writer to alter the work of the first one. And so on. In the end several writers may have had a go. Some Continental films list as many as six or eight writers, with the director's name always displayed prominently among them – often to the fury of the writers.

The process works in very much the same way when a film is based on a novel. It isn't very often that a novelist adapts his own book, because writing for films is a specialised skill. All those detailed explanations of what a character is thinking or feeling have to go. A screenplay consists of what is said and done; the actor provides the emotions.

By the time a novel reaches the cinema screen as a film it may be almost unrecognisable. The completed film of *To the Devil . . . A Daughter* was very different from Dennis Wheatley's original story. The first screenplay by John Peacock was re-written by Chris Wicking, who was thought to be more familiar with the demands of a Hammer film (both names are listed in the credits).

But a typical Hammer film was not what director Peter Sykes wanted to make, so another experienced writer (who remained anonymous) helped out with further changes. Sykes himself re-wrote some of the scenes during shooting. Richard Widmark arrived in England with a list of changes he wanted to make to the character of Verney – which meant more re-writing, because if one character is altered the others who appear with him have to be changed too.

There is one infallible way of discovering how much a film script has been re-written during shooting. Look at a copy of the shooting script. The original version will have been duplicated on green paper; all the changes and additions on pink. So the proportion of pink to green gives the game away.

To adapt a novel for the screen it is not enough to cut out all the descriptive passages and leave the dialogue. It may not be the plot but the author's style that makes it readable. A very long novel may have too many sub-plots and characters to be squeezed into a film of the average running time of 90–100 minutes. You must decide who and what to leave out, and which incidents in the story will be the most exciting and entertaining to look at. Unless it is a classic like David Copperfield – when even the tiniest change will enrage somebody – most directors treat a novel as raw material to be cut about and re-shaped. They want to create something new, not make a faithful copy. The adaptor needs to find out what the director wants and do his best to give it to him.

Every writer would prefer to produce an original screenplay and see it made into a film. But it is much easier for a producer to raise money for a film based on a best-selling novel than for a script that hasn't proved its entertainment value.

To write a film script on spec is to gamble with all the odds against you, unless you already know that a producer or director is looking for a particular kind of story. Even then, you should start off by showing him a 'treatment' outlining the plot and describing the principal characters.

Writing for films is one of the chanciest occupations in a very chancy business. Of course, if you happen to be Alistair MacLean or Robert Bolt or any equally famous writer of box office hits, producers and directors will be queueing up outside your door. Nothing succeeds like success, particularly in the film business.

A completed and approved screenplay is only the first stage that a script goes through.

At screenplay stage, the script will include descriptions of the more important characters and clues to the reasons for their behaviour. The writer may choose to add details like the time of day, the weather (if it affects the plot), or the kind of setting that he has seen in his imagination.

From this completed screenplay the director plans a shooting script. This is a breakdown of the plot into scenes numbered in numerical order. Usually there are two columns: dialogue on the right, a brief description of the set or location on the left. Every scene is numbered so that anything shot out of sequence can easily be put into the right order.

When the director makes changes to his shooting script the details will be given to a production secretary, who will type them out and send duplicate copies to everyone who needs them.

After the final editing of the completed film, a release script is produced. These vary in the amount of detail included, but the best are precise records of everything that is in a film – dialogue, settings, sound effects, background music, and the lyrics of any songs. They will also list the credits as they appear on screen. The reel numbers are included and the footage (the length of film that has passed through the projector by the time a particular scene appears on screen).

Finance

Films cost money. From hundreds of thousands of pounds to millions, depending on the budget that has been agreed as necessary to cover the cost. Naturally, no film can be made until the money is available.

For money to be made available, a film must exist as a promising project. The core of this project is the story.

The story may be based on an already published novel, like Dennis Wheatley's *To the Devil . . . A Daughter*, which has been a best-seller since 1953. It may be no more than an idea on half a sheet of paper. More likely it will exist in the form of a script or a treatment.

If a story has been bought by a major film company the money is ready and waiting, provided the executives don't lose faith in it. An independent producer (someone who has the courage to go ahead without knowing for certain that the completed film will find a distributor) will either use his own money or look for an investor (there may be more than one) who will gamble on the chance of making a profit.

In Britain, raising money is the biggest problem of all. If no investor is interested, a film may die before it is born. Sometimes a film will go into production in a clamour of publicity only to grind to a halt after a few days or weeks. A writer with a head for figures could fill this entire book with horror stories about the films that 'never were' because the money either couldn't be found or ran out before the film was finished.

Even when a film has been made, it may never be shown to the public.

The executives of the distributing company which helped finance it may decide that the film will be a flop, and prefer to cut their losses by leaving the cans on the shelf rather than spend more money on having extra prints made and on publicising the film.

If an independent producer cannot interest a distributor in handling his film, or if he is dissatisfied with the terms he is offered, he may hang on for a better offer that never comes. Or he may eventually sell the film to television.

Even when a film has been taken by a distributor and been shown in one or more cinemas, a producer may decide to withdraw it if he thinks it is not being handled correctly. He may think it is in the wrong kind of cinema with the wrong kind of audience; or he may disagree totally with the way his film is being publicised.

To the Devil . . . A Daughter was never in any danger of being left to gather dust in the vaults. Not that it was all plain sailing. There were delays which caused extra problems when the film went into production.

The film was originally to have been made in the autumn of 1974. By the time the co-production deal with a German company was finally completed, the first day of shooting had been tentatively fixed for early July, 1975. Christopher Lee had, by now, agreed to play Father Michael; but there was a further delay while director Peter Sykes went to the United States to talk Richard Widmark into accepting the role of John Verney. Then the screenplay had to be revised to fit Widmark's screen personality. The first day of shooting was eventually fixed for 1st September 1975.

By now, time was running out for Christopher Lee who was booked to make a film in Canada and had to leave Britain at the beginning of October. On the other hand Richard Widmark could not come to England until the second week of September. So their scenes together would have to be fitted into a period of just over a fortnight.

However, the work of pre-production had been going ahead through August, and the comings and goings of the leading stars were taken into account in the preparation of the shooting schedule.

★ ★ ★ ★ ★ ★

A co-production involving production companies in two or more countries spreads the cost of making a film. It also guarantees that, unless the film is judged to be a failure, it will be shown in each of the participating countries.

In order to make the film attractive to audiences of different nationalities, it is usually part of the deal that actors well known to them will be cast in important roles.

With international stars like Christopher Lee, Richard Widmark and Denholm Elliott topping the bill, *To the Devil . . . A Daughter* had box office appeal everywhere; but some of the supporting roles went to actors better known in Germany than in the U.K.

Co-production deals are very common on the Continent and have been for many years. Since Britain entered the Common Market co-productions involving British companies have become more numerous. It is a way of competing with films made in the United States where the size of the country means that a new film stands a good chance of making a profit before it is sold abroad.

A film goes 'out of the red' when it brings in more money than it cost to make. The money that comes in afterwards is all profit and can go towards making more films. A film made and distributed in one European country stands a poor chance of making a good profit; the more countries involved the quicker it will go out of the red.

David Watkin, Ron Robson, Roy Skeggs

Producer

The producer is the instigator of everything that happens during 'pre-production' – the weeks (or months) of preparation before the cast and crew assemble, and the camera starts rolling.

The producer is the person who controls the money, employs the director, cast and film crew. He approves the expenditure of each head of department, and makes sure the machinery of film-making runs smoothly so that the film 'comes out on budget' (i.e. that it costs no more than was originally planned).

Some – not all – concern themselves with the style and content of the film as well, particularly when they are spending their own money. It all depends on the personalities of the people involved as to whether or not the director takes kindly to this. Tactfully phrased suggestions can be helpful; dictatorial interference may result in an irate director walking off the set and a replacement having to be found in a hurry.

Roy Skeggs, producer of *To the Devil . . . A Daughter*, is one of the tactful kind. Never interfering, but always within reach when needed.

"A good script is the starting point," he says. "Without a good script, you can't have a good film. But it may still have to be re-written and re-shaped because every director has his own approach to film-making."

After Roy Skeggs has agreed the first version of the screenplay with the writer, he engages the director who he believes to be right for the particular type of film. Together, the producer and director then select likely stars and principal supporting characters, a lighting cameraman, an art director, and other heads of department such as wardrobe, make-up, props, and of course, a production manager.

The heads of department, in turn, will decide who they want to assist them. All the crew are freelance, engaged for just the one film at a time.

"Each head of department studies the script in detail and brings me an estimate of what he or she will need to spend." Roy Skeggs may have to ask them to cut down, but, if the budget allows, he will trust their judgment. "Experienced people will usually make economies where they can."

"By now," says Skeggs, "the main reason for my continued existence as producer is to make sure the director has everything and everybody he needs to make the film in the time allowed for by the budget."

Producers will never talk in precise figures, especially when they know they are going to be quoted. In any case, budgets are always expressed in big, round figures. A 'low budget' film averages out at between £200,000–£250,000; a 'medium budget' film (*To the Devil . . . A Daughter* is an example) costs £400,000–£500,000; a 'big budget' production is one costing anything from £1 million upwards. It sounds a lot of money to spend on providing just 90 minutes or so of entertainment. However, if you think of it as being shared out between all the people who have to be employed (including the stars), the equipment, the film stock, costumes, properties, sets, transport and catering, fees for the use of locations, publicity and stills photography, and the hire of the studio, the huge sums do not look quite so huge.

Before the first day of filming, the shooting schedule has to be worked out. This details which scenes will be filmed on which days; and where. No films are shot in sequence, from the beginning of the story to the end, unless they are straightforward recordings of a stage play as it was produced in the theatre.

Two main considerations govern the preparation of the shooting schedule: the availability of actors, and the set or location of the scene to be shot. With *To the Devil . . . A Daughter* the schedule had to be planned so that Christopher Lee could film as many as possible

Call sheet, Screenplay, Shooting schedule

DIRECTOR: PETER SYKES

ARTIST		CHARACTER		D/R	M/U	ON
		VERNEY		CARAVAN	8.30am	ON LOCATION
		DAVID		513	7.30am	8.30am
		ISABEL		517	7.15am	8.30am
RICHARD WIDMARK				518		8.30am ON LOCATION
ANTHONY VALENTINE						
ANNA BENTINCK		Mr. Valentine		502	8.00am	8.30am
STUNT DOUBLE	for			502	8.00am	8.30am
EDDIE POWELL		Mr. Widmark		504	8.00am	8.30am
STAND-INS		Mr. Valentine				
JACK DEARLOVE	for	Miss Bentinck				
RICHARD POORE	for					
JA.. MATTHEWMAN	for					

"Verney's" Jaguar as arranged by Nine Nine Cars on location tine   be adv...

...S.   SCRIPT AND ART DEPT'S INSTRUCTIONS TO INCLUDE:-
TWO "PACT" MEDALLIONS, MATTOCK, BLANKETS, ASHES
... SECRET COMPARTMENT.

THE SCREEN IS BLACK -

and there is total silence for a few beats until with an
exultant roar, part of Carl Orff's "Carmina Burana"
SOUNDS.   The first of the profrane, sacred songs ...
"O Fortuna, Velut Luna".   The choir and orchestra ring
out, rhythmically, louder and louder, becoming more and
more insistent ...

Then, smashing on as the soaring music rises to reach
battering ram proportions, come a succession of both profane
and religious images, in the style of woodcuts, medieval
engravings, line drawings, etc.   These portray various
aspects of the war between God and the Devil ... ...
fight for supremacy on the screen.

Over these - our...

A

HAMMER FILM PRODUCTIONS LIMITED

"TO THE DEVIL A DAUGHTER"

SHOOTING SCHEDULE   2ND WEEK

Date	Sets & Sc. Nos.	Cast	Special Requirem
Monday 8th Sept.	Location Int. Village Church (St.Botoph's Shenley) 10, 11, 101, 103 Night.	MICHAEL HENRY MANSERVANT GEORG EVELINE ISABEL MARGARET BABY CATH...	

of his scenes during the week before Richard Widmark arrived, and could complete his work before the date of his departure for Canada (except for some location filming in Munich in mid-October, for which Lee flew to Germany for a weekend). Other members of the cast had to be similarly fitted in to avoid the need for having them on call longer than necessary.

Then the availability of the actors has to be dovetailed with the availability of sets and locations. Once a set has been built in the studio, or the crew has moved out to a location, it is more practical and economical to film every scene that takes place in that setting.

Production Manager

The production manager is responsible for making sure that everything that is going to be needed during the making of a film is available at the right time. He is the person who gets permission for the use of a location, and he will do this as early as possible before shooting starts.

Ron Jackson, production manager on *To the Devil . . . A Daughter*, knows from experience that you can't be too careful when arranging for location filming. "Even if everything's been fixed months ahead, you still have to go

back a few days before to check. I remember once fixing for a scene to be shot in a road. When we arrived on the day we found they'd dug it up and nobody had bothered to tell us. Then there have been other times when everything has been agreed and the owner has changed his mind at the last moment."

Apart from obvious requirements like equipment, costumes, props and materials for set building, Ron is responsible for the catering and all other amenities required when people are working long hours. These amenities are doubly necessary when the crew and artists are out on location.

He engages the caterers who provide snacks and meals. A light breakfast (very necessary when a working day starts at 8.00 a.m., or earlier); a mid-morning break of sausages, bacon, eggs, biscuits, coffee and tea; a hot lunch; a tea break with sandwiches and cakes. In addition, they must always be prepared to provide food for a supper break if shooting continues after 5.30 p.m., and a late meal if overtime lasts until midnight.

On location, the caterers will arrive in a van that is a mobile kitchen. A converted bus makes a dining room for a sit-down lunch.

Equally important for location filming are the lavatories. A specially converted caravan will have a 'Ladies' at one end and a 'Gents' at the other. They are, of course, of the chemical closet type.

Ron must also make sure that the right number of caravans arrive to provide dressing-rooms for the cast, and for make-up, hair-dressing and costumes. The top stars will be allocated a caravan each so they can sleep, read, go over their lines, give interviews, in complete privacy. The other featured actors will share, two or three to a caravan.

Sometimes Ron has tasks that would seem very bizarre outside the film business. For one of the outdoor scenes in *To the Devil . . . A Daughter*, director Peter Sykes had asked for some butterflies in order to add an attractive touch of summer. So Ron had to arrange it.

The law of supply and demand operates in and around the film industry just as in any other kind of business. There are several firms who provide living creatures of various kinds. Butterfly cocoons (the stage between caterpillar and butterfly when the chrysalis is wrapped inside a silky case) are kept in a deep freeze. Given three days' warning, they can be thawed out and the butterflies will emerge from their cocoons in the normal way.

As production manager, Ron Jackson also keeps a keen eye on all expenditure in relation to the budget. No matter how carefully money has been allocated to each department during pre-production, there will always be the unexpected expense. In consultation with the producer and director, Ron will juggle his figures to help them decide between the relative costs of studio or location filming. A head of department may insist that something is essential and have to be persuaded that a cheaper substitute must be found.

Ron has his own way of keeping all these different tasks under control. "Mostly, I just keep it all in my mind," he says. "You can draw up as many charts as you like but things change so much from minute to minute that a chart is never completely up to date. I keep a record of how much we shoot – how much film footage – and each week the accountant prepares a projected costing of what remains to be done. If we find we're running over the budget then we have to look for economies, like cutting down on overtime or changing a location for one that is less expensive."

"As for all the other things – like caravans and butterflies – that kind of organising ability only comes with experience."

Shooting

The mechanics of a day's filming are simple enough, if anything that involves so many people with so many different skills can be so described. It is the quest for perfection that makes for delays and complications.

In the shooting schedule the screenplay has been broken down into 'takes'. A take is any scene, short or long, which can be filmed and recorded without stopping the camera or changing the lights. Long before the day, the director, art director and lighting cameraman will have agreed the design and colour of the sets to be used, and they will have been constructed.

If, for example, the set is a bedroom, the necessary furniture, ornaments and 'hand props' (any articles that will be picked up by the cast) will be in their places.

The lighting cameraman has decided how the take is to be lit overall and the electricians have mounted the overhead lights according to his instructions. The sound engineer has found a convenient place for his recording equipment where he is out of the way but can see what is happening.

The stand-ins walk through the movements the actors will have to make, so the director can decide exactly how and when he wants the camera to follow them. Chalk lines or yellow strips on the floor ensure that the movements of the cast and camera do not vary, no matter how many times a take is re-shot. If an actor, or the camera, has to move backwards, a batten may be nailed to the floor to prevent either from going too far. In consultation with the director, the lighting cameraman makes final adjustments and positions the smaller lights so the actors' faces are seen clearly and at their best.

When the director is satisfied, the actors will be called to the set for a rehearsal. This may be no more than a rehearsal of their movements and those of the camera and the man who carries the microphone boom (which must never be in shot or cast a shadow, though it does sometimes happen – as sharp-eyed cinema-goers will have noticed).

If the take has little or no dialogue, the director may not need more than this one rehearsal. Otherwise he may decide to have one or more acting rehearsals.

At last, the director decides that no more improvements can be made and he is ready for the take. He informs the 1st assistant director who calls for silence and for the red light to be switched on. When the red warning light is on over the heavy soundproofed doors, no one can enter from outside.

The 1st assistant director's call of "Roll 'em" is the signal for the camera crew and sound crew to start filming and recording. The clapper boy (who usually doubles as assistant focus puller on the camera) steps in front of the lens with the board on which he has written in chalk the title of the film, the number of the scene and the number of the take. He says the words aloud for the benefit of the sound mixer and snaps the two halves of the hinged board together. (This way the start of the take can be easily identified on both sound and vision for the next day's rushes.)

It is usually the director who gives the command "Action". Then the actors do the scene they have rehearsed.

A take may be shot several times before the director is satisfied. He may feel the actors' performances could be improved. An actor may have 'fluffed' a line – which is very easy to do if there has been a change in the script. Or there can be a technical fault; one of the most common is for a hair to get into the lens – magnified on the screen, it looks nearly as big as a tree trunk.

When the director is at last satisfied, he will say, "Print that". The camera operator, the sound mixer and the continuity girl note the number of the take and its length.

Before the next scene can be shot, the director may want covering shots. He may want some of the action to be photographed from a different angle, or an actor to repeat

some of his dialogue in close-up.

The first day of shooting is very like a school reunion, with people who have worked together on other films greeting each other with cries of delight and much swapping of tall tales.

But work comes first. Film people are film people all the world over and the film in production is a baby to be nursed with loving care. All their energy, all their efforts, are devoted to that end.

An outsider visiting a studio is unlikely to realise just how dedicated they are. All he sees is a lot of people sitting around, apparently doing nothing, while a few fidget about mysteriously. Men in overalls sit on packing cases or lean against walls, reading a newspaper or magazine, or doing their pools. A girl is immersed in a book. Another is knitting. People stand in little groups, deep in conversation that is occasionally interrupted by a burst of laughter.

There are reasons why so many of them appear to have nothing to do and all day to do it in. The make-up and hairdressing artists were at their busiest when the leading actors first arrived; now they are only standing by to do any necessary touching-up, or make any changes required for a later scene. Heads of department did their homework during pre-production; provided nothing goes wrong and the director hasn't changed his mind about his requirements for the day's shooting, they are also only standing by in case of an emergency. Others are simply waiting until they are called upon to do whatever their particular job is. Electricians waiting to be told how the next scene is to be lit; stage hands waiting to 'strike' (dismantle) the set when the director is satisfied it is no longer needed; painters who may be needed for a touch-up job; and so on.

The director is now in command and everything is geared to his task of completing the shooting schedule for that day. His concern is

to make sure every take is exactly as he has planned it, subject to any flashes of new inspiration that may come to him. The others are on the spot to provide him with whatever he needs to achieve that end, whether it be the artistry and technical know-how of the lighting cameraman or the 3rd assistant director's speed in bringing the stars from their dressing-rooms.

For most members of the crew, film-making is composed of long periods of inactivity broken by bursts of concentrated effort. Not very glamorous, but there is a magic that holds all these very different people in its spell. Most of them will admit to feeling miserable and lost away from films.

For a period that may be as short as three weeks or as long as a year, these people become as close as a big family. They gossip about each other, exchange confidences about their private lives and loves (and hates), play practical jokes, exchange reminiscences about the funny things that happened during the making of other films, adding to their repertoires with tales of the dramas that occur during the making of the present one.

A visitor is an intruder and noticed immediately. Nobody is happy until they know who they are and why they are there. Very strict rules govern the admission of outsiders. Indeed, some directors (like Ken Russell) will insist on what is known as a 'closed set', which means *No Visitors*. When that happens, not even the most famous show business journalist will be allowed to look on, unless Russell himself issues the invitation.

The reasons for all this are very practical. First, every film calls for a great deal of concentration on the part of the actors, particularly if there are very emotional or dramatic scenes for them to play. The people who work on a set have mastered the art of making themselves invisible. They never wear bright colours. They move silently, hide in shadows, and know when to freeze like statues or look away when a stare might prove distracting. They become, almost literally, 'part of the woodwork'. A visitor who hasn't learned the art of disappearing stands

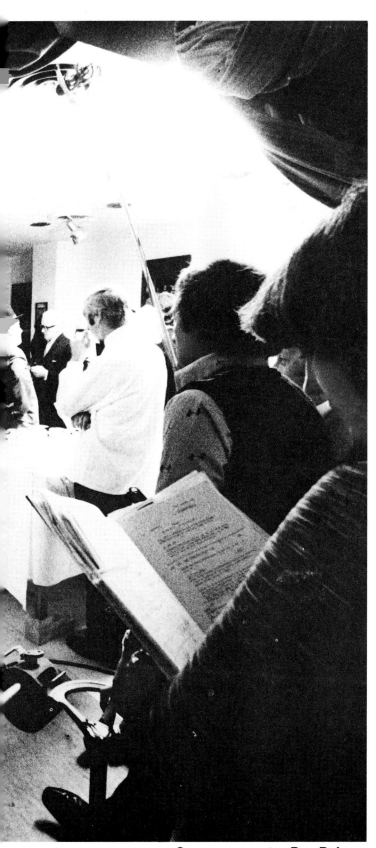

Camera operator Ron Robson

out like a bright light in a cellar.

The second reason is that every studio or location is a tangle of thick cables carrying power to lights, cameras, sound equipment, and machinery required for special effects. Every one is a booby trap waiting for the unwary to trip over it and break an ankle, or – much worse in the eyes of film crews – bring part of a set crashing down. There are boxes and crates, bags containing a carpenter's tools, pots of paint, props that may or may not be needed for the next take.

One innocent false move by a visitor can cause anything from a minor inconvenience to a ruined take. There is no time to spare for avoidable delays when a film is being made, because time costs money. More important still, a false move that disturbs an actor might affect the dramatic balance of the completed film.

Ideally, all directors would prefer to have no visitors at all. But, eventually, a film has to be sold to the public, and visitors from the Press, radio and television are necessary evils endured for the sake of publicity.

Director

Director Peter Sykes is a young Australian who came to England in 1963 and took a training course with BBC Television. He worked on documentaries before turning freelance and directing episodes for series like *The Avengers.* He made his first feature film for the cinema in 1969 (*The Committee*) and his more recent films include *The House in Nightmare Park* and *Steptoe Rides Again.*

Peter Sykes is not a director who shouts and screams. Smiling and soft-spoken, he will listen to suggestions from his cast and film crew and then make up his own mind. One of his first tasks is to help select the crew, starting with the lighting cameraman and the editor. Different people have different attributes and Sykes knows who is right for the type of film being made and who will work well together.

He is also involved with the casting. "I think it's absolutely vital to meet the actors and discuss their roles as they relate to the story, and answer any questions that can be answered before we start shooting."

The director is concerned with all aspects of production. He talks to the art director about the sets and props that will be needed, and to the wardrobe department about costumes. With the lighting cameraman and sound engineers he discussses the equipment to be used. Then there are locations to find, special effects to design, and countless other pre-production details to sort out. "It's a process of building up all the various elements that go into the making of a film. A director has to be able to make quick decisions. You have to know what you want and make sure you get it."

Peter Sykes also believes a director must have some time alone to think. "I like to go into a kind of hibernation and spend as much time as possible by myself, because all I'm concerned with really is the script and how I'm going to put it on screen."

As director, Sykes always goes over the shooting schedule with the producer so it can

Director Peter Sykes

be adjusted if he thinks too much time has been allowed at one stage and too little at another. "When you're doing a lot of shooting outdoors there has to be flexibility because of the weather. I like to make sure there's always something that can be shot as an alternative, so we aren't all sitting about waiting for the rain to stop."

A change in the weather can also disrupt the smooth progress of interior location filming. There is an important scene in *To the Devil . . . A Daughter* which takes place in what is meant to be an art gallery. This was scheduled for shooting in Cork Street, Mayfair, in premises that had once been a hairdressing salon. The cubicles became make-shift dressing-rooms for the four stars; the shop front was decked out with paintings and the sort of furniture you would expect to see in an art gallery in an expensive area like Mayfair. Behind, in the space where ladies once sat waiting for their hair to dry, some 50 or so people were keeping

out of the way while final touches were put to the lighting, with the stand-ins taking up the positions of the stars.

Suddenly it began to rain heavily. The rain itself created no problems, but the heavy clouds darkened the natural light outside so much that the street had to be lit artificially with arc lamps to give the effect of sunshine. This, in turn, affected the lighting of the 'art gallery' which had to be re-thought by lighting cameraman David Watkin. No filming could be done until the afternoon, so cast and crew had to work overtime during the evening to keep the film on schedule.

Peter Sykes confesses he always finds a first day of shooting a traumatic experience. "During pre-production it's all theory and talk. When you start filming, it takes a few days to get the machine oiled so that things run smoothly. The actors are a bit nervous of each other if they haven't acted together before. Even if

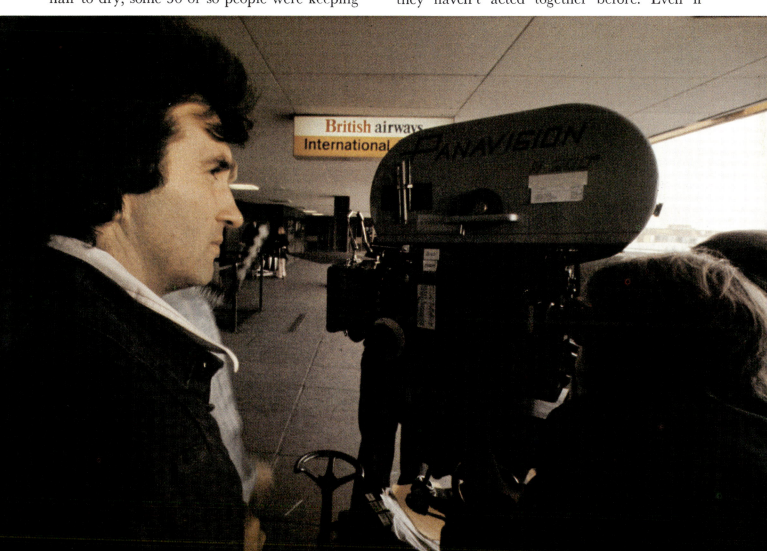

you've held rehearsals, they're inclined to be on edge for the first few days."

Sykes prefers to rehearse the principal actors for at least a fortnight beforehand, but this proved impossible with *To the Devil . . . A Daughter* because they weren't all available at the same time. "I did manage to squeeze in some rehearsing of the scenes between Richard Widmark and Nastassja Kinski. This was particularly important because she is so young and it was only her second film."

Only fifteen while she was playing the highly dramatic role of Catherine, German actress Nastassja developed a strong dislike of Richard Widmark. This was no accident. Believing that the friendly teenager would have difficulty in projecting the fear and hatred with which Catherine rejects Verney's efforts to remove her from Father Michael's satanic influence, Widmark encouraged her dislike of him by remaining aloof and speaking harshly when her performance was too 'soft'. "He taught me a lot," she said afterwards. "He taught me to react properly, to concentrate and to keep my performance under control." Before flying home to the States, Widmark telephoned her to apologise for his toughness and to praise her for doing a good job.

"Once shooting starts, a director must be able to rely on his technicians," says Peter Sykes. "I can see what the lighting looks like; I can look through the camera and watch how and where it moves; I can listen to the sound. But not all the time and certainly not all at once. That's why it's so important to choose the right crew from people in whom you have confidence. Then you can leave them alone to do their jobs while you get on with yours."

There will always be problems which have to be discussed – the lighting, perhaps, or a movement of the camera that makes it necessary to alter the set in some way – but the director's attention must be concentrated on the actors and the look of each scene shot. "You have to have eyes like a hawk, concentrate on what you are doing at the moment, and be

constantly criticising yourself."

A film is eventually put together rather like a jigsaw puzzle. Except that each piece may be shaped and re-shaped from a choice of takes and later re-arranged to form a different pattern. For example, a scene involving two actors will first be filmed as a *two-shot* so that both of them will be seen together on the screen. Then part or all of the same scene may be filmed again with one of the actors in close-up. If the reactions of the other actor are required (or likely to be required) a reverse take of his face in close-up will also be filmed. Perhaps one of them makes a gesture of particular significance, such as pointing to a map or picking up a gun. The director may decide to have a close shot of the actor's arm, or just his hand and wrist, lasting the few seconds that it takes him to complete the movement.

Short takes like these are called *inserts* for the logical reason that they may be inserted either as a means of drawing the audience's attention to something of relevance to the plot, or to add movement and variety to the picture we see on the screen. The principle remains the same whether two actors are seen talking peacefully or an army of extras are engaged in a bar-room brawl.

When all these varied takes are edited together to make a complete scene, the audience must never be consciously aware they are not watching an uninterrupted flow of dialogue and action. Actors must not vary their pace or change their movements. If a gun, or whatever, is picked up it must always appear to be lying in exactly the same place, no matter how many times the action is filmed.

Every scene or insert may be filmed more than once. Each take is numbered and timed but only one will be printed, unless the director has deliberately included a variation that he thinks might prove to be more effective. The printed takes are shown to the director (and anyone else who is interested) at special screenings called *rushes* (in the States, they are known as *dailies*). If nothing needs to be re-shot, the editor will start putting the takes in order according to the director's instructions.

"I build up a scene shot by shot, and that scene is linked in my mind to others. I can end up with thousands of shots, all in my head as well as on film."

All the time he is planning ahead, Peter Sykes knows that once the camera is turning he is committed. The all important thing is that the mood and pace of each scene must be right when he comes to shoot it. If it isn't, he must be sufficiently flexible to change whatever it is that seems to be wrong. "I often reject my first thoughts, because you can always improve things, and experience has taught me that second, third, even fourth thoughts are better."

Whatever changes are made, they must fit in with the montage of shots and scenes Sykes carries around in his head.

An example. "One of the characters in the film is killed. I had to decide whether showing her being killed would give the effect I wanted at that stage of the story, or whether it would be better to reveal the fact that she'd been killed later on. Did I want to introduce an element of horror, or keep it mysterious so the audience wouldn't know the identity of the killer? Once I've decided between these alternatives and settled for showing the murder, do I make the killing explicit or suggest it obliquely, with a shot of a hand holding a knife and sound effects? The final decision doesn't depend on the shock value of this scene alone, but on what comes before, what happens afterwards, and the overall mood of the film."

A scene won't work if a mistake is made by any department. "You might say that small mistakes pass unnoticed; but, unless I and the lighting cameraman and the art director and the actors and everybody else are convinced that everything is as it should be, we can't put

our hearts into a scene and make it believable."

Camera Crew

On screen we see what the lens of the camera sees. What the camera sees is decided by the director; but he does not operate the camera.

The picture may be brightly lit, almost dark, colour, monochrome, garish or subdued. The director decides what atmosphere he wants to create; but he does not decide how the scene will be lit.

Look carefully at the credit titles of any film and you will see about half-a-dozen names listing the people whose job it is to ensure that the picture on screen is exactly as the director saw it in his mind's eye.

For *To the Devil . . . A Daughter* the names read:

Lighting Cameraman	David Watkin
Camera Operator	Ron Robson
Focus	Stephen Smith
Clapper/Focus	Barry Brown
Grip	Peter Woods

In control is the lighting cameraman, second in importance only to the director. This title is still common in Britain, but the more impressive-looking 'Director of Photography' is creeping in from America.

The lighting cameraman plots out the positions of the lights, deciding also their power and whether colour filters are to be used. It is a totally creative task based on his experience and knowledge of film speeds, lenses and film processing. He seldom touches the camera, but may choose to take the camera operator's place during a rehearsal; particularly for a tracking shot to check that there are no unintended changes in the quality of the light.

David Watkin is one of Britain's most famous and admired lighting cameramen, in demand all over the world. His 'trademark' is

Art director Don Picton

his preference for creating the effect of natural lighting, so that an interior set will appear to be lit only by the light coming through the window. He uses reflected light; the beams thrown by the powerful arc lamps will not be directed on the actors, but reflected back from carefully positioned flats, painted white or whatever colour he selects.

Even for an outdoor location extra lighting is usually needed. Real light changes constantly as the sun moves and clouds form. Obviously a scene cannot begin with the sun directly over-head, and then have long shadows appearing suddenly because two takes have been shot several hours apart. Location filming out of doors leaves a lighting cameraman little time for relaxing in the chair that has his name on it. Particularly in Britain where a sunny, cloudless day can become dark with rain clouds within minutes.

Having decided how a scene is to be lit, the lighting cameraman gives his instructions to the 'Gaffer' (the head electrician) who delegates the work to his team of 'Sparks'. When they have finished there may still be changes to be made. One reason could be that there has been an alteration in the set dressing (perhaps to make room for the camera to move in for a tracking shot), and this might have changed the pre-dominating colour. Resilience is a necessary

quality in lighting cameramen and all who carry out their orders.

The camera crew depend on each other. A mistake by any one of them can ruin a take.

As the camera operator concentrates on his task of operating the camera and keeping the picture within its frame, the focus puller keeps it in focus. For a tracking shot the grip grips the steering handle and keeps the wheeled apparatus moving smoothly along the marked lines, bringing it to a halt on precisely the right spot. It's not as easy as it sounds – to keep it moving at just the right speed calls for more than physical strength. A good grip controls the speed at which the camera moves so that it is in keeping with the mood of the scene.

On a low or medium budget production the assistant focus puller may double up as clapper boy. While he learns the work of a focus puller he is responsible for making sure the camera is loaded with the right type of film and that the lens is clean and free of hairs. Simple tasks, but vital. It has been known for a scene to be lost because there was no film in the camera.

When next you admire the perfect picture composition and exquisite lighting in a film made by a great director, remember that its perfections owe something to every member of the camera crew.

Art Director

Art directors are the invisible men of the cinema. Unless a set has to be noticeably unusual or decorative, he has contributed most when we notice it least.

A room is a room. A room in a mansion owned by a millionaire will look different from the bedsitter occupied by a junior clerk. If the art director has done his work well we take that difference for granted. It is only if something strikes us as wrong that we become consciously aware that we are not looking at the real thing.

On location

Don Picton, the art director of *To the Devil . . . A Daughter* has the far-away look of an artist who sees visions created out of his own imagination. But those visions have a practical application. The paintings on the walls of his office represent the first stage in the process of providing the director with sets that will be right for the film.

To be right for a film, a set must help to create the atmosphere of a scene. Or, if the set represents a room in somebody's home, it must reflect the personality of the character who lives there. Don achieves his background effects with the way the set is decorated and furnished, and the choice of ornaments.

He recalls working on the film *The Leather Boys*. "All the characters lived in two streets of identical working class houses, but we made the interiors as different as the families. One house was owned by the grandmother, so we put in Victorian furniture and bric-a-brac. There was a woman who was always out at bingo, so her home looked dusty and untidy. Another was very poor but kept her house spotlessly clean, so we didn't give her many possessions but everything that could glitter was made to glitter. The more you study the script and discuss the characters with the director, the more ideas come to you."

Don is a great believer in getting the right colour for the mood of a film and using it as the dominating colour throughout. But this must be talked over with the lighting camera-man, as well as the director, because lighting affects colour.

Sometimes Don has to do special research before designing a set with unusual features. In *To the Devil . . . A Daughter*, John Verney goes to an ecclesiastical library where rare books are attached to chains. "Even Peter Sykes didn't quite believe such places existed. But I discovered there was one under Lambeth Palace, so off I went with a camera and the production buyer. We photographed it and built a copy – except that we put bigger chains on the books to make them look more impressive."

As an art director, Don Picton regrets the present popularity of real locations. "You have so much more control in the studio. You can position the windows and doors of a set where they'll be most convenient for the actors' moves, the camera can move more freely, and you don't have to worry about noise or the changing light outside. And a real location doesn't necessarily look real. I wanted Verney's flat to be filled with books and bookcases. But the flat we used was too small. I did put all the bookcases in at first, but most of them had to come out again because there just wasn't enough space for them, the cast and the camera crew."

Most art directors of Don Picton's generation (he is in his fifties) started as junior draughtsmen, drawing architectural plans from sketches like those that hang on the walls of Don's office. "You worked your way up to assistant art director and, when you felt sufficiently confident, tried to persuade a producer to give you your chance."

To would-be art directors, Don Picton gives this advice: "Get a basic training first, either as an architectural student or at an art school. You need to be able to do your own painting so that your sketches can be 'read'; you should also have a working knowledge of antiques and the use of colour. And, if you manage to get into films, you must never stop learning."

The art director is the person responsible for how every set will look on the screen. There are a great number of people involved in carrying out his instructions; the bigger the budget of the film, the more of them there will be.

A set dresser buys or hires or borrows such things as ornaments, flowers in vases, and anything that the actors have to handle from a book to a gun. But he may get them from a property master who has a stock of all the props that are frequently needed. A prop dresser collects the props required for a day's shooting and puts them in place.

A construction manager is in command of a team of carpenters (known as Chippies), plasterers, painters, stagehands and riggers who build the sets designed by the art director. These tradesmen could easily find work that would be more regular and secure — possibly better paid — outside the film industry. But like everybody else who falls under the spell, they prefer to work on films because no two days are exactly the same and they can use their ingenuity and imagination.

Special Effects

Very few films are made today without the help of a special effects man. He is the illusionist, the magician, and his magic tricks are not limited to the obvious and spectacular like Dracula being reduced to dust, a man turning into a monstrous entity from outer space (as in *The Quatermass Experiment*), or the blowing up of a monastery (as in *The Face of Fu Manchu*).

These three spectacular effects were all created by Les Bowie, one of the most admired special effects men in the business. Les was responsible for all the special effects in *To the Devil . . . A Daughter*; he created the grotesque devil baby and gave it the appearance of life, and made it possible for Anthony Valentine (as David) to be 'burned to death'.

Effects like these, however, are only the most noticeable and dramatic aspects of Les Bowie's work. Everything in a film is an illusion; even the illusion of continuous action. Every reel of a completed film is composed of single frames which pass through the gate of the projector at the speed of 24 frames a second. What we really see is 24 separate pictures, each slightly different from the last. It is the rapid change from one to another that tricks our eyes into telling our brains that we are seeing moving pictures.

When the whole is an illusion, there is no end to the range of additional tricks that can be played on the viewer in the cause of improving that illusion.

In the days when all films were shot in studios one of the earliest special effects was to take the characters 'out of doors' by positioning the actors in front of a photograph of, say, a country lane. A simple development of this was to project moving pictures on to a translucent screen, which would then be re-shot with the actors performing in the foreground. This created an illusion of movement and speed — when, for instance, an actor was supposed to be driving a car or flying a plane. In old films (and, regrettably, occasionally in new ones) you can recognise this kind of back projection by a shimmering outline of light round the figures in the foreground.

There have been many developments and variations in the art of convincing the audience that the actors are somewhere other than where they really are. Mirrors, miniatures, models, all have their place.

When he was working at Pinewood Studios in the late 1940's, Les Bowie invented a quick and effective method of altering film footage showing a real location to include whatever was required for the story. Say it was a mountain scene that required the addition of a chalet. He would cut out the area where the chalet should be, project the scene on to glass through the camera, then paint the chalet on to the glass. It saved having to go up a mountain to film the real thing.

The increased use of location filming has made this part of Les Bowie's work less important than it used to be. However, new problems spring up like mushrooms to replace the old ones.

For example, Peter Sykes chose a real flat overlooking the Port of London to be the home of the character John Verney. Not every scene could be filmed in the flat because the movements of the camera were too restricted; so 'Verney's bedroom' (precisely the same in every detail) was built as a set in the studio for these extra takes.

Scene 226 'David ablaze'

In the real flat, sunlight shining on the River Thames threw a moving pattern of reflected light and shade up through the window and into the room. Les Bowie was called upon to re-create this effect on the set.

He did it with a large, square, shallow tray containing water on which floated pieces of mirrored glass. As the camera rolled, a few stirs of the water set the bits of glass in motion and a light focussed on the tray did the rest. Quite simple when you know how, like most special effects.

Les Bowie delights in achieving the seemingly impossible by the use of everyday articles like nails, bits of string and lengths of metal tubing. Over the years he has built up a store of knowledge of how certain effects can be achieved economically; but, directors being the sort of people they are, he is constantly being asked for something new. That's when his eyes light up with glee.

When not on the set, he will most likely be found experimenting in his workshop – a wooden hut with shelves and workbench, cluttered with

odds and ends that seem too ordinary to be of any use to a magician. Except, perhaps, for the two large jars of imitation blood, marketed under the punning brand name of 'Kensington Gore'. A dark red and a light red, they can be mixed to produce the exact shade required.

Call Sheet No. 23 was as business-like and factual as any that preceded it. It stated that the location for Tuesday, 30th September, 1975, was St. Botolph's Church, Shenley, and that everybody, including Richard Widmark, Anthony Valentine and Anna Bentinck were to be there ready to start work at 8.30 a.m.

For most members of the crew and cast it was a normal day's work, when the only discomfort might be caused by bad weather. It was in fact quite a chilly day, and there were forecasts of sudden heavy showers of rain.

But it wasn't the possibility of getting cold and wet that frayed tempers. Neither was it because of being inside a church that there

wasn't as much laughing and joking as usual.

The clues to the cause of this mood of unrest were to be found in the call sheet: "Carbon dioxide fire extinguishers to be on hand; Nurse Peta Walters to stand by; two firemen to be in attendance." And under the heading of 'Artists', Stunt Double Eddie Powell was listed as required to be on location by 8.30 a.m.

Even without checking the shooting script, everyone knew that this was the day when Peter Sykes intended to shoot the scene where David (Anthony Valentine) is consumed by fire – a manifestation of the satanic power of Father Michael.

Scene 226 ("David ablaze") was not the first to be shot; a number of scenes with Richard Widmark and Anthony Valentine had to be completed first. All this took time.

Between takes, a tall man paced up and down the aisle of the church. He would occasionally smile and speak to someone he recognised, but nobody disturbed his concentration for very long. This was Eddie Powell, the stuntman, familiarising himself with the distance he would have to travel enveloped in flames, and how much clearance he had between the pews that flanked the central aisle. He had never before performed such a potentially dangerous stunt in such a confined space.

Special effects chief Les Bowie clothed Eddie in a fire-proofed coverall, worn beneath a suit that matched Anthony Valentine's. He covered his face and head with a fireproof mask and wig. In theory, at least, Eddie could see through transparent 'windows' rather smaller than his eyes.

There would be no re-takes or extra covering shots for this scene. You don't chance your luck more than once when you set a man on fire. Three cameras instead of one were positioned to capture "David's agonised stumbling" from altar to nave. Between them, their lenses viewed most of the interior of the church, so only those members of the crew who could hide themselves on the floor behind a pew were allowed to remain.

Les Bowie daubed Eddie's clothes with an oily, highly inflammable liquid. With the cameras rolling, he set fire to the stuntman and stood back. Eddie remained where he was for a moment till he was well and truly alight. Then, with arms outstretched, he began to stumble down the aisle, turning round and round as he went. He was required to do this as part of the action, but it was learned afterwards that – as soon as the flames covered his face – he could no longer see where he was going. Only his sense of direction kept him on a fairly straight course. As it was, he struck an upright metal lampholder at the end of one of the pews, lost his balance, and only a last courageous effort to keep on his feet brought him close enough to the spot where he was supposed to fall – thus saving the take.

Without a second's delay the firemen rushed forward to extinguish the flames.

Soon Eddie was being helped to his feet to be examined by the nurse. A bit singed and scorched, but otherwise fine.

Some of the words expressing relief may not have been used in quite the context they are normally heard in a church, but they were as heartfelt as any hymn of thanksgiving.

On screen, Scene 226 is spectacularly effective. No wonder. It wasn't far short of being totally and tragically real.

Wardrobe

Dressing the cast of a film calls for a lot of organising ability, as well as a knowledge of period clothes and a flair for matching modern dress to the character.

The Wardrobe Supervisor for *To the Devil . . . A Daughter* was Laura Nightingale, who started to work in film studios 20 years ago. The film was *Ivanhoe* and Laura's task was to make at least three complete 12th century costumes every week. "It was very hard going in those days," Laura recalls. "But meeting stars like Clark Gable and Robert Taylor was like

entering a magic world. I take stars more for granted now, but I still feel the magic in the business."

As wardrobe supervisor, Laura Nightingale's job starts with the script and a list of the cast, excluding the extras who provide their own clothes. From the script she will learn what sort of people the characters are (young or old, fashionable or dowdy, rich or poor), and she will discuss with the director any particular facets of a character which need to be emphasised.

"For example, in this film the character played by Honor Blackman is a woman living with a man younger than herself. So I chose clothes that suggested she was trying a little too hard to be youthful and trendy." Busy actors can never spare much time for wardrobe and there's always a slight panic getting them fitted out. "You get used to it and provided you keep cool it all gets done. The important thing is to plan ahead so none of that precious time is wasted."

The studios no longer keep a huge collection of period costumes that can be used over and over again. The cost of cleaning, repairing, preserving and cataloguing makes it uneconomic to store what can easily be hired from a costumiers. For modern dress, Laura keeps a book in which she notes the addresses of useful shops and the type of clothes they sell. "More often than not, I can go straight to the right shop for the right clothes. This cuts out a lot of time-wasting trial and error."

Once all the necessary costumes have been selected (with stand-by replacements for those likely to get torn or dirtied, or worn by doubles), Laura draws up 'dress charts' detailing what clothes will be worn by whom, and in what scenes. This is not only an easy reference for what will be needed for a particular day's shooting, but it also prevents mistakes in continuity. When scenes are shot out of sequence even someone with a good memory for detail can forget exactly what was worn two weeks previously. Naturally, the continuity girl keeps

her eyes open for this kind of mistake, but by the time she spots it the day's work has already begun. Then, unless it is possible to 'shoot round' the scene (i.e. move on to another shot on the same set in which that character does not appear), everybody has to wait until the error has been corrected.

"Once I've got the dress chart worked out, I try and stick to it. Of course, there can still be last minute changes of cast, or the director may have second thoughts and move a scene indoors (or vice versa), which will affect the clothing. But you can always cope with sudden alterations if you've planned ahead."

★ ★ ★ ★ ★ ★

The Wardrobe Supervisor has the responsibility of choosing the clothes to be worn by the cast; buying, hiring, and occasionally arranging for special costumes to be made.

The Wardrobe Master (or Mistress) takes care of the costumes while a particular film is in production; mending, washing, ironing – or, if they are meant to be dirty and ragged, keeping them at the right degree of ragged grubbiness. It is also the wardrobe master or mistress who takes the clothes needed for a day's shooting to the stars' dressing-rooms.

Eddie Boyce, wardrobe master on *To the Devil . . . A Daughter*, is the friend and confidant of stars all over the world; he takes them as he finds them – which is often at their worst. A temperamental star in a bad mood on a bad day will meet his match in Eddie, who was a regimental sergeant major during the war and can give as good as he gets.

While a film's in production a very close personal relationship develops between an actor and the wardrobe master. The way the latter behaves can make all the difference between an actor starting the day contented or miserable.

"In a sense I've already done my job for the day before shooting starts. I've studied the call sheet before hand, and I know which actors are working and what clothes they're going to wear. So everything is ready and waiting for them. But I'm around all the time in case of an emergency – whether it's just a button that's come off or something gets damaged and has to be replaced in a hurry."

Emergencies don't often catch Eddie unprepared; experience has taught him to predict when they are likely to occur. He reads the script carefully, noting all the places where an actor may get wet or dirty, have his clothes stained with artificial blood, or have a fight in which something he's wearing may get torn. Then he makes sure he has identical replacements should the scene have to be shot again. "A wardrobe master who kept an entire film hanging about on location while he went off to find another blue shirt, say, would soon be out of a job." But that isn't the end of it. "Even when I think I've got everything I'm going to need, I read the script over and over again, just in case there's some tiny detail I've missed."

The amount of running repairs, pressing and cleaning Eddie may have to do depends very much on the character being played. Obviously, someone who's meant to be very clean and tidy needs·more looking after than somebody who's playing a tramp. But even a tramp mustn't suddenly become more ragged and dirty in the middle of a scene.

Sometimes the simplest problem turns out to be one of the most difficult to solve. The starched clerical collars worn by Christopher Lee as the infamous Father Michael are the perfect example. Eddie had to search around for an old-fashioned laundry that could wash and starch them properly.

Another hazard the wardrobe department has to cope with is the star who prefers to wear his or her own clothes. "It can cause us a lot of trouble," says Eddie. "He's probably had them made in a special material. Maybe he feels more comfortable in them – he knows they make him look good and that helps him to give a better performance. I understand how he feels, but it's no joke having to find an exact copy."

During production a director may suddenly want to play a scene a different way, calling for a double to take over in a fight or a car crash. Somehow, the wardrobe department has to find a suit that is a duplicate of the one the actor is wearing.

Sometimes stars will bring clothes from abroad and take them back when they go home. After they've gone, the director may decide he needs a covering shot – a back view of the star going through a door, for instance. It would cost too much to bring the actor back just for one small scene that could easily be done by a double. Again, it's the wardrobe department that has to find clothes that won't give the game away.

Hairdresser

Jeanette Freeman didn't start out with a burning ambition to work in films. She did the normal training of a hairdressing apprentice, and was working in a salon when her production manager husband begged her to help out on a film that had no hairdresser. She liked the work and the people, and never returned to the salon.

But the job does have its drawbacks. "If you come into the business all starry-eyed, it soon gets knocked out of you. A working day that starts in a cold, draughty studio at seven o'clock in the morning and doesn't end until about seven in the evening soon wears the gilt off the gingerbread."

Some days can be very boring. The artists have their hair done before shooting starts and, theoretically, Jeanette has no more to do except wait about in case a hairstyle gets disarranged. Often this isn't really necessary, but she knows it helps to give the actors confidence if they feel they are being looked after and made to look at their best.

"There are times, of course, when I have to do the very opposite and make them look at their worst. Funnily enough, professional

Props

Honor Blackman

Kensington Gore

actresses don't mind this because it's all part of their job. It's the men who are inclined to be more difficult and fussy about how they look."

Period hairstyles create special problems for Jeanette, especially those of the fairly recent past. "There are a lot of hairstyles which look very unflattering to present day eyes. For instance, in this film there's a flashback to 25 years ago. If you look at photographs that were taken then most of the people look a good deal older in them than they do now." Jeanette has to adapt the styles to make them more flattering, but without changing them too much from the real thing.

The only part of her early training that is of no use to Jeanette is hair colouring; and her skill with 'perms' is used only on her friends. But she has had to learn about the way our ancestors wore their hair and how to do emergency repairs and alterations to wigs. A job she enjoys particularly is making a double's hair look the same as that of the star he or she is impersonating.

When a film is made on location in a foreign country, the hairdresser goes as part of the crew, taking everything she is likely to need. "There can be no popping into the high street salon to borrow half-a-dozen rollers when you're in the middle of a desert or halfway up a mountain," laughs Jeanette.

Make-up

A film star's day when he is on call starts very early and begins in the make-up department.

The artificial look, with even the mouths of the men heavily lipsticked, went out when faster film made very bright lights unnecessary. A straight make-up will be simple: a dust of powder to remove shine, a light foundation such as most women use to make their skins look smooth and flawless. If signs of tiredness or age need to be concealed, every brand of good cosmetics includes creams and powders to lighten dark bags under the eyes or give a more youthful glow to the cheeks. Most of the tricks for making a woman look more beautiful were discovered by the make-up artists who worked for film studios, and later passed their secrets on when women wanted to look like their favourite star heroines.

If a character has to age a few years in a film, it is equally simple to darken the bags and wrinkles, leave the cheeks pale and brush on a brownish shadow to make them look hollow.

It is only if a character has to be aged by many years, has to be made to resemble a real person, needs to look scarred, or to have a grotesque appearance, that make-up needs to be heavy. Every make-up artist has his own favourite materials for adding the bags and sags and changing the shape of a face. Clay, rubber solution, and many of the new plastics are used.

But heavy make-up is the exception, not the rule. Most actors are chosen because they are – or look – the right age. For example, in *To the Devil . . . A Daughter*, Anthony Valentine wore no make-up at all.

George Blackler, the chief make-up artist on *To the Devil . . . A Daughter*, has no set rules; he works instinctively out of his long experience. He reads the script and discussses the principal characters with the director and producer, absorbing their ideas. Then he creates what he sees in his mind. "It's rather like playing a piece of music and giving it your own interpretation."

He has done make-up for many Hammer horror films. "I enjoy them because I have to use my imagination. Withered hands, withered heads, scars . . . that sort of make-up is very interesting and a lot of fun to do."

George was a little disappointed to have no horrific faces to create in *To the Devil . . . A Daughter*, but he was kept busy keeping each actor's make-up in line with the suspense of the story. Under stress, people go pale or perspire, or flush with anger. If they die in the story, they must look dead.

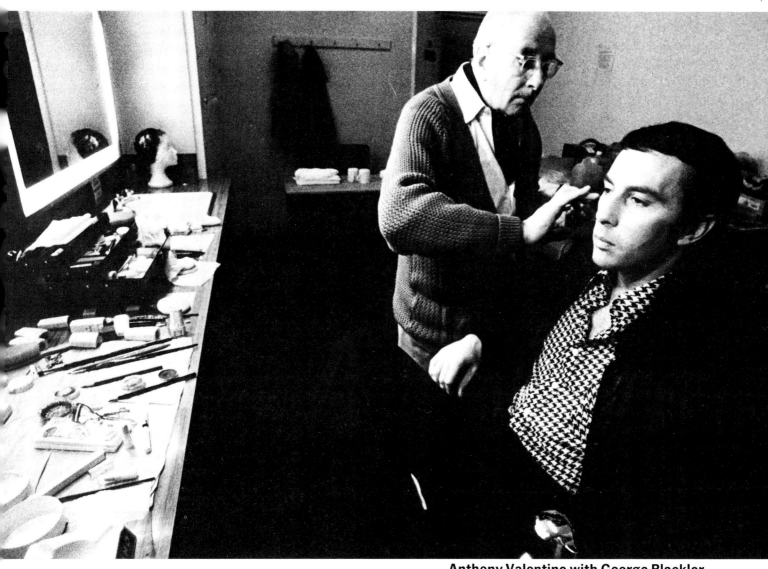

Anthony Valentine with George Blackler

The great moments for any make-up artist come when an actor's face has to be totally changed; perhaps to make him resemble an historic character, or to add fifty years or more, or to create the face of a monster.

It isn't only human beings who need the help of a make-up artist. Frank Westmore, the youngest of the six famous Westmore brothers who practised their art in Hollywood when the studios were churning out films, recalls how when he was nineteen, and still learning, he was told there was a big job awaiting him. It certainly was a big job – he had to paint an elephant called Mabel a darker shade of grey. Not just once, but every day while the film (*Beyond the Blue Horizon*) was being shot.

Actors

The glamour of the cinema is focussed on the stars. The glitter of stardom can make the most ordinary man or woman seem special. Only the passage of time proves whether the glitter is gilt or untarnishable gold; the extra something that makes a real star survive for decades, blinding us to wrinkles, sags, paunches, punch-ups and bad publicity.

Not all actors will admit to wanting to become a star. The fame and money have to be paid for in loss of personal freedom; the intrusions into your private life, the interviewers who probe into your most secret thoughts. But given the chance of stardom, how many of us could turn down the possibility of being able to demand several million dollars for a few days work?

Robert Redford was paid two million dollars for ten days' work on *A Bridge Too Far*; Sean Connery received one million dollars for eight days on the same film; and Marlon Brando accepted two million dollars for twelve days' work on *Superman*.

To make that kind of money a star must be 'bankable', which is the term used for someone whose name on a poster will ensure box office success all over the world. They are expensive to employ because the size of the profit on a film depends on them. Clint Eastwood, Charles Bronson, John Wayne, Paul Newman, Steve McQueen, Barbra Streisand and Elizabeth Taylor are all bankable stars.

It may be tough at the top, but it can be much tougher down below. Only the established character actors never hear the wolf howling outside the door. Not depending on their looks and sex appeal, they can go on for ever and always be in demand.

A popular series on television can give an actor enough standing to enable him to haggle over the fee; but the majority, who are out of work more often than in, get the basic minimum of £20 a day.

This would be good money if the actor worked every day while a film was in production – but shooting schedules are planned to have the supporting actors on call for the

Richard Widmark

30

Christopher Lee

shortest time possible. Extras are paid £12.50 for an eight-hour day; stand-ins get £12.90; doubles, £14.90. There are additional payments for overtime, night work, weekends, and so on. But even with these it rarely adds up to very much.

Christopher Lee is an international star who is more of an international star than most, because he speaks French, German, Spanish and Italian. So it is his own voice that audiences hear in films made on the Continent or when a British or American film is dubbed into those languages.

But he has never forgotten what it was like to be unknown and unwanted. He looks back at his early days of struggle with some amusement.

"From 1947–1957 I played any character I got a chance to play, anywhere in the world. In a film called *That Lady*, made in Spain, I had a few lines as the Captain of the Guard. I also played masked grooms, devilish assassins at mid-night, and various other weirdies with and without beards, with and without masks, on horses and off horses. I ran up and down precipices. I did some stunts on a horse by a river which ended with me disappearing under water."

The reasons why he remained unknown were summed up by a casting director when Christopher Lee was under contract to the Rank Organisation: "We can't use you because nobody has heard of you, you don't look English and you are six-foot-four." No British male star wanted to be dwarfed by such a tall and handsome young man.

It is well known that Christopher Lee's career in films took off after he played the Creature in Hammer's *The Curse of Frankenstein*, though it was, of course, as Count Dracula that he established himself as a King of Horror. He is proud of the care and thought that went into the performances that won him this title, but dislikes it being used carelessly by people who forget the many very different characters he has played.

"There is too much careless thinking about

films that are usually called 'horrors' – though I prefer the word 'fantasy'," he says. "To make a supernatural or horrific character really convincing, actors must give more – not less – attention to the subtleties of emotion. Draçula, the Creature and the Mummy all share the quality of sadness. They are not entirely responsible for their actions; they are driven by an inner compulsion, an evil force, and they experience the loneliness of evil. They must be pitied as well as feared, and this is a challenging combination for an actor."

In 1973, Christopher Lee announced that he would no longer appear in horror films and would give all his time to the many other kinds of films he had been starring in all along. Dramas, comedies, thrillers, westerns and mysteries.

In spite of this, he allowed himself to be persuaded to play Father Michael in *To the Devil . . . A Daughter*.

"It is not a horror film in the sense that the term is normally used. It is terrifying, but not fantasy. Behind the story lies a dreadful truth. The cinema is a reflection of life and the perfect medium to show what lies beneath the surface attraction of dabbling in witchcraft. As an actor, what better reason could I have for appearing in a film that will, I hope, shock people by showing them how much of this does go on and how terrible it is."

Christopher Lee made these comments when he was shivering in the damp coldness of an autumn morning on location on a hilltop in West Wycombe. The scene to be shot was Father Michael's final confrontation with John Verney. He had just spent over an hour 'walking through' his movements for the benefit of the camera and sound crews. In his priest's robe and thin-soled shoes, he was denied the comfort of the anoraks and thick boots of the technicians and the other non-acting members of the team.

No matter how much special treatment a star may get when he is working on a film, there will always be times when he has to endure as much – if not more – discomfort than anybody else. Busy stars like Christopher Lee can't even afford to catch cold because snuffles and sneezes and red noses are not what they are paid to have.

Stardom is not all limousines and VIP treatment. When special effects man Les Bowie set the wind machine going to create the effect of an invisible and mighty force coming to the aid of Father Michael, it was Richard Widmark and Christopher Lee who stood in its icy path.

Stars, supporting players, bit part actors, even the non-speaking extras, all have the satisfaction of appearing in front of the cameras. But there are other actors who are just as necessary in the making of a film but are never seen by a cinema audience. They are the stand-ins. You will not see the name 'Chick Fowles' in the credit titles of *To the Devil . . . A Daughter*. Yet his name is well known to many world famous stars who might sometimes have given less than their best without him.

Chick is a stand-in: Denholm Elliott's stand-in on *To the Devil . . . A Daughter*. In the past twenty years he has stood-in for over a hundred star actors, including Albert Lieven, Alexander Knox, Terence Morgan, Fredric March, Ian Bannen and David Niven.

His job is to stand where the actor will stand, and move as the actor will move, while a scene is being lit and the camera crew and boom operator are rehearsing their own movements. This enables the actor to come to the set fresh, with all his energy kept in reserve for his performance.

A stand-in's working day can be very tiring; all toil and no glory. It can also be very tedious; but, like everybody else involved in the making of films, Chick takes too much pride in doing his job well to get bored. He will put himself out to do anything that may help the film he is working on to be a success.

Apart from the obvious essentials of being

German actress Nastassja Kinski

the same height and roughly the same build as the star, a good stand-in will be in demand because of his forethought and readiness to do more than just stand here and go there. "For example, a good stand-in will think to wear similar clothes to those his star is wearing in the scene," Chick explains. 'This helps. the lighting cameraman."

"It's essential for a stand-in to watch all rehearsals so he knows the moves his star has to make. If any changes are made when I am standing-in for him, I will go and tell him what they are."

Although a stand-in is never in front of the camera during a take, he will sometimes stand behind and read the other character's lines when only one actor's half of a scene is being filmed. "Having been on the stage for many years, I like to think I read the lines well enough to help the actor with his reactions."

Chick admits that being a stand-in has its frustrating moments. "Particularly when I see somebody in a supporting role I could play myself." But the job also has its consolations. "It's a way of earning a living that's much better than being forced to take a job outside the business. At least you've still got the excitement of trying to do your best for the film, however small your contribution may be. You get so much more out of a job if you're not working just for the money."

A star appearing in a film may also have a double, who may or may not be a stuntman.

A stuntman performs the dangerous feats that could injure the star. It is not always caution or well-justified cowardice that prevent stars from doing their own stunts, but the hard economic fact that a broken leg (or worse) would delay the completion of the film, or even cause it to be abandoned.

There are stars – sometimes called 'physical actors' – who insist on doing their own stunts, but the budget of a film has to be big enough to cover the cost of a heavy insurance. Steve McQueen, James Caan, Clint Eastwood, Burt Reynolds, Jean Paul Belmondo, Jimmy Wang Yu, George Lazenby and James Coburn have all done their own stunts in recent films. So has Christopher Lee, who describes his death scene in *Airport '77* as the most dangerous stunt he has ever performed.

This does not mean that the stuntmen are likely to find themselves out of work. These 'physical actors' have helped to make action films so popular that directors have been forced to dream up bigger and better stunts that no actor in his right mind would attempt.

However, a double is not always a stuntman. He may be an actor who looks sufficiently like a star that he can take his place without being spotted by sharp-eyed audiences. After his cast has dispersed, a director may find during editing that he needs covering shots of a star looking away from the camera, or walking out of a room. With the right clothes, make-up and hairstyle, a double making a brief appearance will be accepted by the audience as the real thing.

Or if the script calls for the star to be seen in long shot in a foreign location, it is cheaper to employ a double than fly out a highly-paid star.

A new use for doubles has cropped up in recent years since the acceptance of nude scenes in films. Actors and actresses who prefer not to strip naked – and are sufficiently established to be able to refuse without being replaced by someone who doesn't argue – will have a double to take over at the crucial moment.

It is not unknown for stars to be watching a completed film at a premiere and be startled by a nude scene, inserted without their knowledge. Some have been known to sue the film company. But, if the double has a better shaped figure, a star may prefer not to give away the secret.

Continuity

One of the most difficult people to talk to during the making of a film is the continuity girl. Not because she's unapproachable, but because she is busy all the time.

The importance of the continuity girl is self-evident. Even the most uncritical member of a cinema audience will notice a character who goes through a door with his hat on and appears on the other side with it off. (Or, as happened in a film recently, starts a scene wearing a helmet and ends it wearing a cap.) The most splendidly acted scene will be wasted on an audience that is giggling because the bottle of sauce on the table has suddenly vanished, or an empty cup has been magically filled.

Originally the continuity girl was only responsible for making sure there were no gaps or mistakes in the action and dialogue; she was there just to help the director remember where he'd got to. Now she is expected to keep an eye on hair, make-up, props, costumes; in fact, everything that could be accidentally changed. "Then there are things like bruises," says Sally Jones who looked after the continuity on *To the*

Continuity girl Sally Jones

Devil . . . A Daughter. "I have to watch the time sequence of scenes so that a bruise is seen to fade naturally and doesn't come and go."

Like everybody else directly concerned with what will be seen and heard on screen, Sally starts off by studying the script. She reads it over and over again till the story and characters are clear in her mind.

She insists that a good memory isn't an essential qualification for a continuity girl. Far more crucial is the ability to differentiate between what is important and what isn't. "It would be hopelessly difficult to remember everything that happens in a take, but you must be able to recognise the things that relate to the scene that comes before or after. For example, if an actor has to repeat some of his dialogue so that the editor can cut to a close-up, I must be able to remind the actor that he turned his head to the left or right on a particular word."

An integral part of Sally's job is to time every take that is printed, but she uses her own discretion and ignores anything that she knows will be cut in the editing – such as a long take of an aeroplane landing, which will never reach the screen in its entirety.

"When you've been doing this job for a few years you come to know instinctively what is right and what is wrong. The only way to learn how to be a continuity girl is to be one and make your own mistakes."

3rd Assistant Director

3rd assistant director is a posh title that has replaced 'Tea Boy'. The job means a lot of running around and knowing where to find everybody. Friendly and smiling and always busy, Roy Stevens works hard, makes himself liked, and stores away everything he sees and hears about the art of making films. For Roy hopes to become a director one day.

He left school with this ambition, but knew nobody who could help him by proposing him for membership of the right union (the Association of Cinematograph Television and Allied Technicians – known as ACTT). So he had to go by a very roundabout route to get where he is.

He kept himself by working in a factory and took an evening job as a cinema doorman. This enabled him to join NATKE (The National Association of Theatrical Television and Kine Employees) and, after a while, he took advantage of this by becoming a stagehand at the MGM studios. Luck was on his side when he was knocked out by a piece of wood falling on his head and was allowed to transfer to the camera department. What he learned there qualified him to work in a film laboratory; this in turn qualified him to join the technicians' union and get accepted as a 3rd assistant.

Roy knows it will not be easy to achieve his ambition; 3rd assistants seldom become directors. They move up to 2nd and 1st assistant, but the next step is usually to production manager, or location manager. "I want to get to 1st assistant and then try to get a break as a director. You have to rely a lot on luck. Learn all you can and hope that when the time comes somebody will remember you, and take a chance."

The luck of being the right person in the right place at the right time is a recognised factor in every show business career. But determined people like Roy make themselves ready to answer the knock of opportunity.

Meanwhile, he works at his present job which he describes as "keeping information travelling around the set." He carries messages, makes sure that the caterers have arrived, and that they know the time of the next break and the number of meals to be served. He silences any chatter during a take, and summons the actors when the director is ready for a rehearsal.

One day, he hopes, there will be somebody doing the job for him.

Stills Photographer

The photographs of scenes from films that appear in newspapers and magazines to illustrate an article or review are always referred to as 'stills'. They are not lifted from the film itself, but photographs taken by a special stills cameraman during rehearsals.

The one member of the team who is not directly involved in the actual making of a film, the stills cameraman is, in a sense, always in somebody's way. "I'm a necessary evil," says Ray Hearne, the stills cameraman on *To the Devil . . . A Daughter*. "The main part of my job is to cover the story of the film in pictures, so I'm dodging about with my camera all the time the actors are rehearsing. Nobody likes this, but it has to be done."

His job looks easy enough, as he clicks away with his camera. But there's more to producing good stills than just photographing everything in sight.

Every newspaper and magazine has a picture editor who selects the photographs to appear in that publication. He could receive twenty stills and reject them all as unsuitable because they are not the sort of pictures his readers want to look at. If you compare the photographs that appear in *The Times* with those published in a less serious newspaper like *The Sun*, you will see why a stills cameraman like Ray Hearne has to provide a varied choice of material.

A still may also be ignored by a picture editor for the mundane reason that it will not reproduce well. The dark, atmospheric photograph which looks so beautiful on the glossy page of a magazine would be a blurred smudge in most newspapers.

While trying to take pictures that will satisfy the very different needs of every kind of publication, the stills cameraman also has to cope with the problems particular to the film he is working on. In *To the Devil . . . A Daughter*, a lot of dark colours were used. These looked perfect on the screen but were difficult to reproduce in black and white.

"No matter how hard you try, you can never please everybody on this job. The director wants stills that capture the mood of the film, the publicity people want stills that will please the Press, and the cast wants pictures that make them look at their best. You can't win."

Although the stills cameraman is not actively involved in the making of the film, he may be asked to take photographs for the benefit of other members of the crew. If a set has to be re-built, or a location reproduced in the studio, photographs taken by the stills cameraman are used to record every detail that must be re-created exactly.

He will also take any photographs that are needed to dress a set: a framed portrait on a desk or mantelpiece; the photograph of 'John Verney' that appears on the cover of his 'latest book'.

A stills cameraman since 1936, Ray Hearne has a library of stills to remind him of every film he has worked on. A unique souvenir of forty years as "a necessary evil".

Sound

Sound may be recorded at the time of shooting or recorded later. Peter Sykes prefers to record all the dialogue as it is spoken by the actors and only fall back on post-synchronised speech if the conditions on location have made good recording impossible.

'Impossible' is not a word in Dennis Whitlock's vocabulary. He was the Sound Mixer on *To the Devil . . . A Daughter*. The title refers principally to the work he does in post-production, mixing dialogue, sound effects and music. During filming, he concentrates on getting a perfect recording of the dialogue.

For any scene in which the cast remain in one place with a limited amount of movement, he sits at the controls of a very sophisticated tape recorder while the boom operator keeps the microphone at the right distance from the actors.

Recording sound perfectly is a highly skilled and technically complicated job that can only be correctly described and understood by sound engineers. Over-recording (too loud) causes distortion. Under-recording (too low) produces a hissing noise. These are errors that Dennis Whitlock would never make because they are the mistakes of a beginner. He will be concentrating on controlling the quality of the sound as it is affected by the accoustics of the set or location.

Films frequently require dialogue to be recorded when the actors are in a car that is moving. The easy way is to have them say the words so that the lip movements are there, and get them to re-record later. But, provided the director is in agreement, Dennis Whitlock will hide himself on the floor of the car with a miniature tape recorder and achieve a perfect recording.

For every take, the sound that is recorded is identified when the clapper boy says the number of the scene and take, and claps the two halves of the board together. When the time comes, the right recording can easily be matched

to the right pictures.

Putting sound to a film is a complicated process. Dialogue, sound effects, music, are recorded separately and will be mixed during the period known as post-production.

Human brains and ears can select what we hear. We can be in a noisy crowd and 'shut out' everything except what our friends are saying; or eavesdrop on a conversation going on at the next table. Properly positioned microphones are selective up to a point, but they cannot distinguish between dialogue and extraneous noises.

Some directors make a feature of this, believing it is more realistic if we can't hear more than one word in three for the hubbub that's going on while the actors are speaking.

Others, particularly Italian directors, record no dialogue as it will be heard when the film is completed. Everything said at the time is recorded (often in a babble of several languages

or different Italian accents) simply as a guide for when the dialogue is post-synched or dubbed after the film has been finally edited.

Most British directors take the middle path, recording all the dialogue that can be successfully recorded during shooting and adding post-synchronised speech only when absolutely necessary.

Post-synchronised dialogue is often confused with dubbing. Post-synchronisation is when an actor has already said the lines and is required to record them again to match his original lip movements (and whatever emotions he put into them). Among the best kept secrets of film making are the occasions when the actor is not available for some reason and somebody else imitates his voice.

Dubbing is when the dialogue is translated into another language. Ideally, a new script will be written that retains the sense of the original and uses words that will fit the lip movements. Then the dialogue will be spoken by experienced actors who have learned both the skill of matching the lip movements and the art of matching the emotions of the characters as well. But this takes time and costs more money than is usually made available. Unfortunately, far too many films are dubbed cheaply and badly and these are the ones that are noticed.

The dialogue is only part of the soundtrack; sound effects have to be added. Only if there is some unusual sound will it have to be recorded specially, as there are libraries of sound effects on disc and tape. Footsteps, pistol shots, doors opening and shutting, car and aeroplane engines (and it must be the right engine noise for the particular model because there will always be someone in an audience who will notice an error); in fact, every sound that is not dialogue spoken by an actor.

Then there is the music track. The chosen composer knows the type of film and will have discussed with the director the kind of music he has in mind. The composer sees the film, possibly as early as the rough cut, and writes the melody of the theme (or themes) that will accompany as much, or as little, of the action as the director decides.

Once approved by the director, the melody is orchestrated and musicians booked for recording sessions. They will record anything from a long piece lasting several minutes to a snatch of music lasting a few seconds – or a single chord.

The composer for *To the Devil . . . A Daughter* was American Paul Glass, described by Peter Sykes as "one of the most highly qualified musicians I've ever met."

Editing

The film editor for *To the Devil . . . A Daughter* was John Trumper, who started his career in the cutting rooms in 1943. His editing credits include *Up The Junction, The Long Day's Dying, The Italian Job, Entertaining Mr Sloane,* and *Get Carter.*

If nothing else was involved, a film editor would simply put all the director-approved takes in order and splice them together. In fact, this is only the first stage in editing. The rushes are put together in the order that they appear in the shooting script. This is known as 'assembly'.

Then comes the *rough cut.* It is the result of the director and editor's first thoughts about how each scene will be compiled from the various takes that were printed. It is recognisably a film with a story that can be seen (but

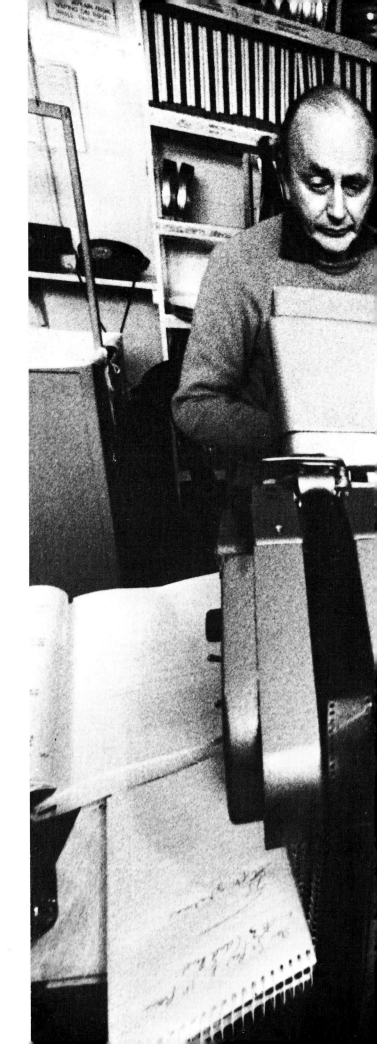

but, unless he has himself been an editor in the past, he must rely on the editor's experience, skill and instinct to a great extent.

Editing is all trial and error. Every director and editor have to face the same problem; they know the story inside out, in all its variations, and have seen every take over and over again. There may come a time when they can no longer see a film with the eyes of someone seeing it for the first time.

In the heyday of Hollywood it was the accepted next-to-last stage in editing to have a sneak preview. The film would be shown in a public cinema to an audience that was not expecting to see it. Their reactions would be noted, and when they came out they would be handed a list of questions to be answered. Their reactions and answers might be discouraging, but there was still time for the film to be turned into a hit.

The sneak preview went out of favour, but it is coming back because it is useful. *The Godfather*, one of the big box office successes of recent years, was sneak previewed and over 180 new edits and cuts were made to the film before the premiere.

The fine cut, also known as the cutting copy, is then sent to the laboratories where the negative is cut to correspond exactly. It is from this master print that further positive prints are taken. The very first of these will be studied by the director and lighting cameraman to check the quality of the colour. Sequences may be too dark, too light, too blue, too yellow, etc.; every amateur photographer knows how colour printing can vary. This print may be sent back to the laboratories several times before the director and lighting cameraman are completely satisfied.

It is at the fine cut stage that the composer and sound editor are at their busiest. The sound editor cuts the sound track to match the film footage.

The magnetic sound track (on tape) is added to the master negative as optical sound to produce the married (or combined) print that is the master negative.

When a film goes on release in the United Kingdom, and is sold abroad, a very large number of positive prints will have to be made. These are produced by an electronic system computerised to the exact grading of the print approved by the director and lighting cameraman, and the sound should be reproduced with equal precision. In theory, that is. In practice, the prints distributed are not always up to the standard of the original.

Publicity

The most exciting, the funniest, even the greatest film of the year could be on at your local cinema. It could be there right now. But unless you know it exists, want to see it, and go to see it, all the money, time, talent and skill that went into making it, will have been wasted.

Clever publicity may sometimes trick us into seeing a film that is far from great, but without publicity we would miss a lot. The building up of interest starts before a film goes into production, with news items and photographs of the stars (and the prettiest girls) supplied to newspapers and magazines by the unit publicist.

Unit publicist is a job that demands patience, tact, and the ability to be firm with the stars as well as the journalists who want to interview them. Mike Russell, unit publicist on *To the Devil . . . A Daughter*, is one of the best liked and respected.

Mike's job is to get the maximum publicity with the least interruption to the making of the film. Like walking a tightrope, it looks easy when you know how but it takes a lot of doing. It means sorting out the professional sheep from the star-struck goats, all demanding exclusive interviews; juggling with call sheets to find times when a star will be off the set, and matching those times with the busy working days of press, television and radio journalists; talking temperamental stars into being interviewed; collecting biographical details and good

stories to be included in press handouts; choosing the stills that are most likely to get published by the many different kinds of periodical.

Designing the poster

On top of all this, the publicist may find himself giving up what little remains of his private life to being anything from the travelling companion to the drinking partner of a star who is far away from home and cannot go out for an evening without getting mobbed by fans.

Meanwhile, the full publicity machinery is beginning to tick over. Posters are being roughed out, but will not be approved by the director of publicity and his colleagues until the film can be seen by them. Just in case the completed film differs from how it was originally imagined.

The same goes for trailers, which are made by one of the companies who specialise in this work. These are mini-film productions in their own right, starting with a script which is

approved when the rough cut of the feature is ready.

To the Devil . . . A Daughter was distributed by EMI Film Productions Ltd., a subsidiary of the larger company which also controls the chain of ABC cinemas. The director of publicity is David Jones, who has devoted nearly 50 years of his life to publicising and promoting films. What he doesn't know about the job of selling films to the public isn't worth knowing, and he is as enthusiastic today as he must have been when he first started. "My budget for everything involved in a publicity campaign is 10% of the production cost of the film. That is to say, anything from £25,000 to £250,000."

Everything means everything. Trailers, posters, printing costs, television and radio commercials, receptions, parties, premieres, special preview screenings. If it is decided to bring stars or the director to this country for interviews, the cost of their flights, hotels, telephone calls and spending money, will all come out of the same budget. "If a film gets off to a really good start then it isn't too difficult to persuade the distributors to provide another £10,000. But at the time of launching a film, we keep inside the budget."

As the West End opening date approaches, the first preview screenings for critics are for those representing magazines which go to press two, or even three, months ahead of publication date. Then come the screenings for television and radio producers, researchers, critics and presenters of programmes.

The type of film decides what other previews may be needed – the music press, fashion editors, policemen, doctors, sportsmen, or whatever. These previews are held in one of the many small private cinemas in and around the West End. EMI have their own which they would normally use.

There are also 'talkers' screenings' for selected groups of the general public: late night

shows for people working in hairdressing salons and pubs who, if they like the film, will recommend it to their customers. Sometimes there will be special film shows for the winners of competitions run by newspapers or one of the local radio stations.

David Jones is a great believer in the value of word of mouth recommendations. "If your publicity campaign is big enough you will always sustain a film for two out of seven days. Then it's on its own. If the word gets round that it isn't as good as the advertisements say it is, it will flop. If it's recommended, it will build up."

The most common day for a film to open in the West End is a Thursday, and it will have been shown to the National Press critics earlier that week. Their reviews can, but not always, affect the box office returns.

Some films just open. Others have premieres attended by the stars and other famous personalities – Royal Premieres, Charity Premieres, or Invited Audience Premieres. A good cause may benefit, and the publicists hope that some of the photographs taken will appear in the press. There are long faces to be seen next day if a big news story crowds the premiere off the pages, or if there is a newspaper strike.

Cinema managers outside the West End of London are encouraged to make special efforts to publicise a film locally. They are sent a list of suggested campaigns, but the more enterprising like to think up their own and a prize is awarded each year for the best.

Good film music will help to sell a film – and, in turn, the film will help to sell the album. A hit number is a bonus all round because it will be played so often on the air, and there have been films that have been successful for that reason alone.

If some films seem to get more publicity than others it is usually because they were more expensive to make, and the budget for the publicity is correspondingly higher. Which is logical, because the more a film cost to produce, the more tickets need to be sold for it to make a profit. David Jones insists that every film gets its fair crack of the whip.

"We have a ruling that the publicity department must get behind every film. You must divorce your own opinion from your efforts. I've known films we've loved that have gone badly, and films we've disliked that have gone well. The film business is not one for backing your own opinion."

Last Word

By the spring of 1977, about 14 months after the London opening, *To the Devil . . . A Daughter* had been seen by at least 1½ million people in the United Kingdom. And it was still going strong.

But home sales represent only a very small percentage of the money the film was bringing in. It had been sold all over the world except for countries like South Africa, Red China, the Communist bloc, Cuba and Finland, where all horror films are banned.

Apart from the German-speaking countries of Austria, Switzerland, East and West Germany, reserved for the German production company, there had been no pre-agreed distribution outside the UK. Every sale to a foreign country – from USA, Canada and Latin America, to Thailand, Cyprus, Syria and Jordan – was negotiated separately by EMI.

This is regarded as a very satisfactory financial return for a medium budget production. Particularly as it is a timeless story that can be re-issued for many years to come.

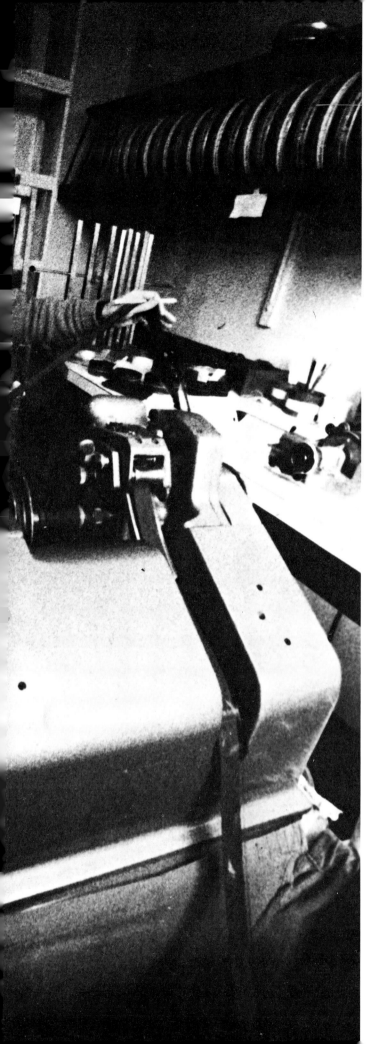

not heard) by executives of the production and distributing companies, and by publicists planning how to sell it. Generally speaking, the rough cut will be from half-an-hour to three-quarters of an hour longer than the completed film.

The next stage is the *fine cut*, when every take is in precisely the right order as agreed by the director and editor.

But what is precisely the right order? The art of editing is finding the answer to that question. Even if the director doesn't decide to change the sequence of the scenes that tell the story, there are still many alternative ways that individual takes can be fitted in.

Let's take a simple example. An actor makes a threatening gesture. Is it going to be more dramatically effective to cut immediately to his victim's reaction of surprise and fear, or should he continue his violent action until it is the moment to show his victim's body on the ground? Multiply that decision by the hundreds of times that the director has taken covering shots, reverse shots, one-shots, two-shots, inserts, etc., and it becomes obvious how much the pace and mood of a film depend on how it is cut together.

Even the actual development of a story can be changed without any new scenes having to be shot. Imagine a story in which Fred robs a bank after he meets Alice and falls in love with her. Put the scenes of the robbery before he meets Alice and you can suggest that his love for her turns him into a reformed character. Or the robbery could be broken up into brief scenes to be used as flashbacks, suggesting that Fred is tormented by his conscience.

In films more complex than this imaginary drama, when the thoughts and reactions of the characters are more important than their actions, the alternatives increase in number along with the complexities of their mixed emotions.

It is the editing that finally makes or breaks a film. The director will work with the editor, discussing, viewing, changing this take for that;

Glossary of Film Terms

Bit player	*An actor with a few lines of dialogue.*
Boom	*An adjustable rod used for suspending a microphone above the actors.*
Call sheet	*A list of cast members needed next day, and any specially required personnel and props.*
Cameo	*An important but supporting role played by a star who may appear once only.*
Changeover	*The procedure of switching from one cinema projector to another, as one reel ends and another begins, at 20 minute intervals.*
Chippy	*A carpenter.*
Covering shot	*A take shot as a possible alternative, as an aid to continuity in editing.*
Dissolve	*When one scene merges into another.*
Dolly	*Wheeled platform on which the camera is mounted.*
Double	*Someone who resembles a star and can take his or her place on screen.*
Dubbing	*Adding dialogue in a different language from the original.*
Dupe	*A copy of a print taken from a positive print.*
Extra	*Someone who has no dialogue and appears in crowd scenes.*
Fine cut	*The final edited version of the film before sound is added.*
Footage	*The length of a film measured in feet; 90 feet equals 1 minute of running time.*
Frame	*A single picture; cinema films move at a speed of 24 frames per second to give the illusion of continuous movement.*
Gaffer	*The head electrician.*
Grip	*The man who grips the handle of the camera dolly and guides it into position.*
Insert	*Short take to be later inserted in a scene to focus attention on an action or object.*
Location	*An exterior or interior setting away from the studio and not purpose-built.*

Looping	*An alternative word for dubbing; describes the method used when two ends of a short length of film are joined, enabling a scene to be projected repeatedly.*
Magnetic sound	*Sound recorded on magnetic tape.*
Matte	*A special effect creating the illusion that the actors are on location.*
Mixing	*The putting together of dialogue, music and sound effects.*
Movieola	*A trade name for a machine used in editing which enables the editor to view single frames.*
Negative print	*The Master Print from which positive prints are obtained.*
On call	*Term used to indicate that an actor or member of the crew is available on a particular day.*
Optical sound	*The standard sound process; photographed on to the release print from the magnetic sound on the negative print.*
Positive print	*A print of a film as it will be projected in a cinema.*
Post-synching	*The re-recording of dialogue in the original language, in studio conditions, to ensure audibility.*
Props	*Movable items used on a set; also the name given to the person responsible for putting them where they should be.*
Quadrophonic	*See Stereophonic.*
Rack	*The line separating two frames.*
Reel	*1000 feet of film (10 minutes); for projection in cinemas it is normal for two reels to be spliced together as double reels.*
Release script	*The final screenplay of the completed film; usually listing all credits, sets, music, sound effects, camera angles and footage.*
Reverse shot	*A take repeated, but with the camera facing the opposite way.*
Rough cut	*The first stage of editing, when all takes are assembled in sequence (also known as Assembly).*

Rushes	*The first screening of all the previous day's takes that the director selected for printing.*
Scene	*Any continuous action in one setting, including all takes.*
Set	*A purpose-built setting constructed in a studio.*
Shooting schedule	*The breakdown of scenes to be shot out of sequence for the most economical use of actors, sets and locations.*
Shooting script	*The screenplay broken down into takes, numbered in order, with brief descriptions of sets and locations.*
Slate	*Another name for the clapperboard.*
Sparks	*An electrician.*
Splice	*When two ends of film are cemented together.*
Stand in	*Someone of similar build and colouring to a star who takes his or her place for camera and lighting rehearsals.*
Stereophonic Quadrophonic, etc.	*Multiple soundtracks giving additional perspective to the sound in a cinema auditorium.*
Supporting actor	*Member of the cast with an important but not starring role.*
Take	*A scene of any length filmed without stopping the camera.*
Teaser trailer	*A very short trailer (15 – 30 seconds) which may not include any extract from the film.*
Trailer	*A short film specially produced for use in cinemas to advertise a coming production.*
Travelling Matte	*A special effect creating the illusion that the actors are on location and in movement.*
Voice over	*Any dialogue heard when the actor or narrator is not seen to be speaking.*

Cast

John Verney	RICHARD WIDMARK	Eveline de Grass	EVA-MARIA MEINEKE
Father Michael	CHRISTOPHER LEE	David	ANTHONY VALENTINE
Anna	HONOR BLACKMAN	Bishop	DEREK FRANCIS
Henry Beddows	DENHOLM ELLIOTT	Margaret	ISABELLA TELEZYNSKA
George de Grass	MICHAEL GOODLIFFE	Kollde	CONSTANTIN DE GOGUEL
Catherine	NASTASSJA KINSKI	Isabel	ANNA BENTINCK

Credits

Produced by	ROY SKEGGS	Assistant Director	BARRY LANGLEY
Directed by	PETER SYKES	Casting Director	IRENE LAMB
Screenplay by	CHRIS WICKING	Sound Recordist	DENNIS WHITLOCK
Adaptation by	JOHN PEACOCK	Sound Editor	MIKE LE-MARE
From the novel by	DENNIS WHEATLEY	Camera Operator	RON ROBSON
Director of Photography	DAVID WATKIN	Continuity	SALLY JONES
Editor	JOHN TRUMPER	Make-Up	ERIC ALLWRIGHT
Production Manager	RON JACKSON		GEORGE BLACKLER
Art Director	DON PICTON	Wardrobe Supervisor	LAURA NIGHTINGALE
Special Effects	LES BOWIE	Hairdressing Supervisor	JEANETTE FREEMAN

**A HAMMER/TERRA
ANGLO/GERMAN CO-PRODUCTION**

Technicolor®

Distributed by EMI Film Distributors Limited

Length: 8,280 ft. approx.   **Running Time: 92 mins. approx.**   **Certificate: X**

**The Publishers wish to thank
Hammer Film Productions Limited for their
co-operation in producing this book.**

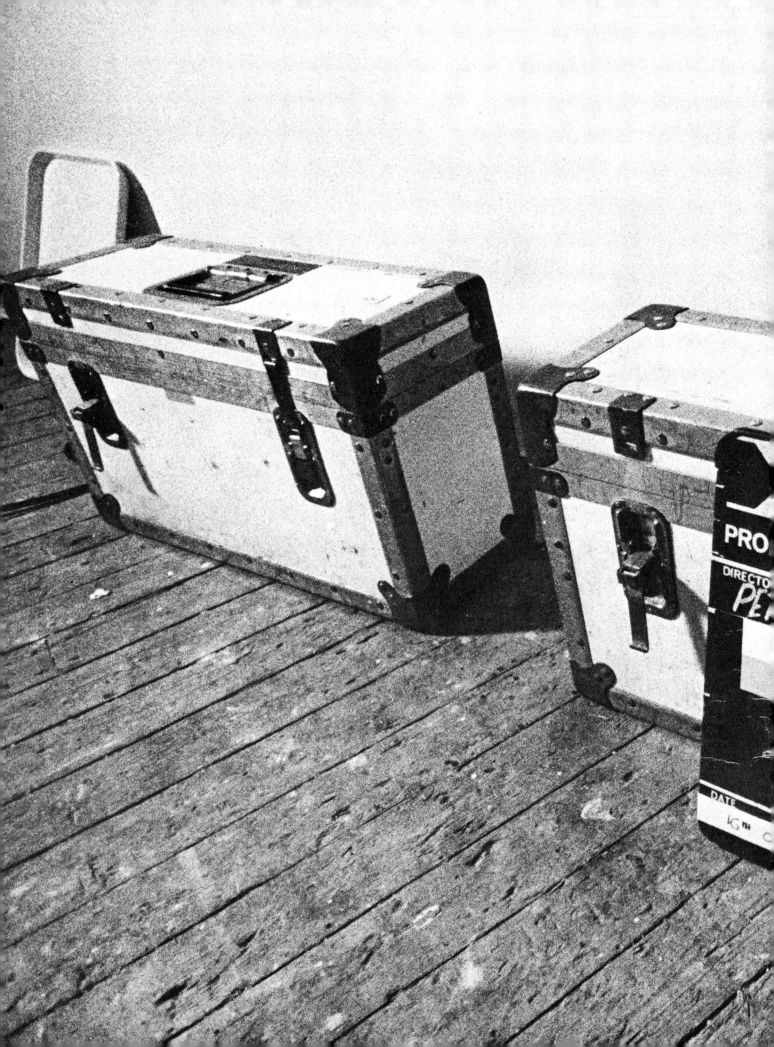